Shifting into High Gear

Transforming an Ordinary Life to Experience God's
Extraordinary Intent for Your Life

J. W. Jasper Jr.

sermonto**book**
.com

Sermon To Book
www.sermontobook.com

Shifting into High Gear / J. W. Jasper Jr.
ISBN-13: 978-1-945793-65-3
ISBN-10: 1-945793-65-1

I dedicate this book, first and foremost, to my Lord and Savior, Jesus Christ, for His omnipotence and the way He has equipped me with the insight and tenacity to write this book.

To my wonderful parents, the late Rev. J. W. Jasper Sr. and Mrs. Mammie Lee Jasper, who provided my foundation and never gave up on me.

To my amazing wife, Lady Angela, who is my prayer partner, faithful companion, and as she declares, my greatest admirer. I am grateful to God for blessing me with a spiritual wife who supports all my endeavors.

To my wonderful children: Lacy Robins and her husband, Jarvis Robins; Xavier Bloodsaw and his wife, Arielle Bloodsaw; Jana Rodgers and her husband, Terrance Rodgers; Javonta Jasper; John Jasper III; and Shalishia Valentine.

To my grandchildren: Jayden Robins, Jaycie Robins, Jermarion Rodgers, Zoey Bloodsaw, and Zaria Bloodsaw.

To the members of my church family, for their continuous love and faithfulness to New Light Baptist Church.

To my other partners who have supported my endeavors: Rev. James Tarver, Tammy Tarver, Tammie Foy, Vonda Malte, Janet Harvey, Monica Edmond, Deshawn Oaks, Nedra Oaks, Prentice Denkins, David Phillips, and all those who made this book possible.

CONTENTS

Stuck in First Gear

Have you ever driven a manual car with a stick shift? When the car is in first gear, it can only go so fast. Depending on the vehicle, it might not go above ten miles per hour before it starts roaring and grumbling. Some will go as fast as twenty miles per hour, but then they max out and won't accelerate any higher. In first gear, some cars lurch around, stopping and then starting with a bump.

You can get where you want to go in a vehicle stuck in first gear, but it won't be fast, and it might not be a very smooth ride!

Many of us feel that we're stuck in first gear in our lives. We may feel as though we are at a point in our lives where we want to get somewhere. We see Christians around us who seem to be moving forward in their walk with God, and we want that for ourselves—but it seems out of reach. Maybe your personal life feels like it's always a mess, or maybe you know there has to be more to life, but you just aren't experiencing that passion or joy.

For some of us, we see these problems in our churches.

We struggle to welcome new people, because the people we already have just aren't welcoming. Bickering and arguing have replaced love and grace. And every time the pastor wants to try something new, there are a dozen people saying that it won't work.

If this sounds like something you see in your life, this book is for you. Be warned: I'm going to tell you what the Bible says, and I won't cut you any slack. God has so much more for you than what you have been living! But if you can take an honest look at yourself and apply the principles I lay out for you, I truly believe that you can shift into high gear and get where you need to be.

What will it mean for you to shift into high gear? It means you will:

- Move forward, instead of backsliding into sin.

- Have a character and a life transformed and remodeled by the Holy Spirit.

- Live free of unnecessary, weighty baggage.

- Be free to forgive, be generous, and be grateful.

- Build bridges for now and for the future within your church.

I've included a workbook section after each chapter to help you better understand and apply these truths to your life. These sections offer questions to help focus your attention on your life and begin to think through and apply what we've discussed in each chapter. Feel free to journal about these questions elsewhere, or use the space provided right here in this book.

Shifting out of first gear takes you further down the road, faster and more smoothly. Doesn't that sound like a better option than lurching forward at a first-gear pace?

CHAPTER ONE

Stop Backsliding

*Let the wicked forsake his way, and the unrighteous man
his thoughts: and let him return unto the Lord, and he will
have mercy upon him; and to our God, for he will abun-
dantly pardon.*

—Isaiah 55:7 *(KJV)*

Remember when you first came to Christ? All your
sins were wiped away, and you were welcomed with open
arms by a loving Father. Wasn't that a glorious feeling?
You set out from that moment ready to take on the world
and help others find their way out of the dark and into His
light (1 Peter 2:9).

But things got harder after that. Life wasn't different,
even though you were. Despite your good intentions, sin
crept back in: the coarse language, the extra drinks, the
thrill of gossip, the unhealthy pursuit of riches, the stingi-
ness, the apathy, the careless relationships. They tiptoe in,
one at a time, in increments, marring your new-found
walk with Jesus just a little more every week.

That "mountaintop" experience with God is one you have to maintain with discipline and hard work. Rather than standing on top of the mountain and getting to hang out in God's chalet, you found that recovering those heady feelings is a daily climb.

And some days you climb well. Some days you read your Bible and turn your problems over to the Holy Spirit right away. On those days, you can handle it when your boss bites your head off or the driver in front of you steers like a maniac.

On other days, though, the climb feels like it's too much. You don't make any forward progress, and instead, you find yourself sliding backward. If we don't deal with it right away, it becomes a habit—and ultimately, a sin problem. As Proverbs 14:14 says, "The backslider in heart will be filled with his own ways, but a good man will be satisfied from above."

Jesus told the church in Ephesus, "But I have this against you, that you have abandoned the love you had at first. Remember therefore from where you have fallen; repent, and do the works you did at first" (Revelation 2:4–5 ESV). Some of us have become crippled by our backsliding, and we don't even realize how it crept upon us. All we know is that we are now stuck in first gear and we can't get where God wants us to be.

Protect Your Mind, Heart, and Mouth

The good news is that backsliding is something you can prevent. When you know what to look for, you can stop before it ever becomes a habit. God doesn't want you to be stuck. He wants you moving ahead in your walk with Him and in becoming more and more like His Son. When we remain in Jesus, we move forward in faith: "I am the vine, you are the branches. He who abides in Me, and I in him, bears much fruit; for without Me you can do nothing" (John 15:5).

Backsliding begins in our minds, moves to our hearts, and then comes out through our mouths. The Bible tells us how important it is to keep our minds on the right things. As Philippians 4:8b (NIV) encourages us, "if anything is excellent or praiseworthy—think about such things." The apostle Paul, who wrote this letter, knew that our thoughts are the gateways to our hearts.

The wise writer of Proverbs knew the same: "For as he thinks in his heart, so is he" (Proverbs 23:7). We must only spend time thinking about excellent or praiseworthy things. As the contemporary adage goes, "Garbage in, garbage out."

Jesus Himself put it this way: "But those things which proceed out of the mouth come from the heart, and they defile a man. For out of the heart proceed evil thoughts, murders, adulteries, fornications, thefts, false witness, blasphemies" (Matthew 15:18–19).

What we say comes from our hearts, and what we feel comes from how we think—including what we think *about.*

You've seen this happen before. You meet somebody new at church and the person seems so nice. You might shake his or her hand and even laugh together about something the first time you meet. Before long, you're Facebook friends and you enjoy the pictures the person posts of his or her family.

But then someone who has known this person for years comes up and tells you, "He or she cheated on his or her first spouse." Even though you haven't had any problems with this person yourself, you start thinking about him or her differently. And before long, you start noticing little things he or she does, and you mention it to other people when you talk about the person. In no time at all, you begin avoiding him or her at church, and you may even block him or her on Facebook. Eventually, every time his or her name comes up, you jump in with some other stories you've heard about the person.

What did you let into your mind? Nothing excellent or praiseworthy, that's for certain. We do this in little ways all the time. The bill collector calls and asks for us, and we tell whoever answered the phone to lie and say that we aren't home. We tell ourselves that it's not a big problem—or even really a sin. But once we start thinking that these things are fine, we are changing our hearts, and in no time at all, more and more lies are popping out of our mouths.

Wickedness Is a Dangerous Road

Some people think that if they don't go out of the house and cheat on their spouses, then they aren't choosing wickedness. They look around at everyone else and see another man's sin clearly, but then they ignore their own. We can easily spot the tiniest blemish on someone else's church clothes while ignoring the enormous stain on our own (Matthew 7:3).

But wickedness isn't just the glaring hole in others; unfortunately, it is in the heart of every human. Romans 3:23a states that "all have sinned"—none of us is exempt.

You must understand that wickedness can take you where you don't want to be. It starts in the mind, goes to the heart, and then moves into the outer parts of your life. You know there are television shows or movies you shouldn't watch. They are full of wickedness, yet you may think, *"Oh, I can watch this. I'm not the one sinning, so it's fine for me to be entertained by this."*

Over time, we start shifting our ideas of right and wrong away from what the Bible says and toward what the media says. Our children watch these things and start acting like the people on television. We absorb this wickedness into our hearts, because we let it into our minds.

Sometimes this happens through the people with whom we choose to spend our time. I know I've found myself acting one way with one set of friends and another way with a different group. I let their words and actions into my mind, and those things begin to change what I believe in my heart. Then, before I realize it, words are coming out of my mouth that reveal what is really happening inside of me.

Take a moment to think about the people whose words get into your thoughts on a regular basis. Are these words excellent or praiseworthy? Now, I'm not saying to cut them out of your life entirely and refuse to speak to them in public. Rather, be aware that a poisonous tongue will impact you in a negative way. Don't let those individuals get going on certain topics. Excuse yourself if they start ranting and complaining. Choose to spend time with people who speak goodness into your life.

While you're at it, choose wisely what you feed your mind. What do you watch on your television, computer, tablet, phone, or at the theater? What books, magazines, blogs, or websites do you read? Consider the sources of your news, entertainment, education, opinions, and perspectives. Who is influencing those who influence you?

It's important, because what you think matters. Filter everything through the worldview of Scripture, and let the Holy Spirit be the gatekeeper of your mind.

Good News

If you feel that you are backsliding, there is good news. God is waiting with open arms to forgive your sin and draw you back to the life He has always intended you to lead. Hosea 14:4 says, "I will heal their backsliding, I will love them freely…." I don't know about you, but that is a promise I hold on to tightly.

The thing is, there aren't any perfect people in the world; we are all sinners. The only perfection is that which Jesus has given us through His death and resurrection. We live in an imperfect world and can't expect perfection in an imperfect situation.

Life is messy. I am a sinner, and you are a sinner. Every person with whom we come into contact is a sinner. We are going to hurt each other, step on each other's toes, and bruise each other's feelings. Sometimes this happens intentionally; sometimes it takes place by accident.

God is already there, forgiving us as soon as we turn to

Him. However, He asks us to do the same for others and forgive them (Matthew 6:14; Mark 11:25).

Remember the story of the prodigal son from Luke 15:11–32? A young man went to his father and asked for his inheritance—even before his father's death. We all know the son's request is unorthodox. We witness this phenomenon in our own time as well, when a son believes he has reached manhood and wants to do things his own way, rejecting his parents. The son, therefore, decided it was time to leave his father and live on his own.

The father agreed to give the boy his inheritance, which we can assume was a huge amount of money. The boy went out and spent the money partying and living a carefree life. When he was left penniless and starving, the boy decided to go back to his father and ask him if he could work as his servant.

You know the end to this story. The father welcomed his son back with forgiveness, joy, and love. Jesus told this parable to represent the way that God welcomes us back after we've strayed from Him.

No matter how bad the situation looks, God will receive you back to Him. Isn't that wonderful news?

Change Your Character

If you're going to live for God, you've got to change your character. It's simply part and parcel of becoming like Jesus. We want to become as filled with the fruit of the Holy Spirit as He was—with love, joy, peace, patience, kindness, goodness, faithfulness, and self-control

(Galatians 5:22–23 ESV). But, as fruit doesn't grow over-
night, our transformation doesn't happen instantaneously
either; it takes a lifetime to build character.

However, it's the little choices we make all day long
that determine who we are when the big decisions come
along. How do we make good choices? By following the
example of Jesus, the example of other godly believers,
the wisdom of Scripture (the Proverbs in particular are full
of practical guidance). Make those godly decisions daily
and you will ensure that who you are next year at this time
is the person you want to see looking back at you in the
mirror.

There are many things you can do to shape your character, and I'm going to discuss several of these in the
following chapters. For now, I want to leave you with one
big idea to help you start thinking about who you want to
be.

My wife and I bought our oldest daughter her first car.
Let me tell you, she was very excited about it. After she
had it a few months, she gave me a ride one day. I climbed
into the passenger seat, and when I did, I saw a list of rules
she'd written and taped to the dashboard. Her list included
having her riders pay her gas money so that no one would
take advantage of her, instructions on how to behave so
that she wasn't distracted while driving, and so on.

When I asked her what the list was about, she said,
"Daddy, this is my car. These are all the dos and the don'ts
you have to follow if I let you ride with me. Daddy, you
bought this car for me. It's a special gift, and I don't want
anyone messing it up."

Think about that in terms of your life. God has given

you forgiveness, and He wants to bless you tremendously. What rules should you stick to the dashboard of your life? The rules for you and everyone around you? With what will you choose to surround yourself to keep from getting hurt and wasting your precious gift?

We want to remain true to our First Love (Revelation 2:4–5). We want to move forward, out of first gear, into a steady track of growth. Just as you'd never put diesel in a car designed for unleaded gasoline, take care to put the right mental fuel into your heart and mind. To keep from sliding back into first gear, we must be intentional and strategic about what we put into our minds and, therefore, our hearts. Pursue the character of Christ by abiding in Him and you will find yourself moving ever forward.

WORKBOOK

Chapter One Questions

Question: How would you define *backsliding*, and what are areas in your life where you are prone to it?

_____

_____

_____

_____

_____

_____

_____

_____

_____

_____

_____

Question: How can you safeguard your mind to stop backsliding before it starts?

_____

_____

_____

_____

_____

_____

_____

_____

_____

_____

_____

Question: Think about the people who have the greatest influence in your life. Are they influencing you toward growth or regression in your walk with Christ?

_____

_____

_____

_____

_____

_____

_____

_____

_____

_____

_____

Action: What character qualities do you want to grow in? Pick three and then set goals for each one.

Chapter One Notes

_____

_____

_____

_____

_____

_____

_____

_____

_____

_____

_____

_____

_____

_____

_____

_____

_____

_____

_____

_____

_____

CHAPTER TWO

Let the Holy Spirit Remodel Your Life

But the Helper, the Holy Spirit, whom the Father will send in My name, He will teach you all things, and bring to your remembrance all things that I said to you.
—John 14:26

There are a number of home makeover shows on television right now. A couple decides to buy an old, dilapidated house and then pours huge amounts of money into making it brand-new again. It goes beyond painting and new carpet. The windows are changed, and walls are knocked down. There's a new roof, and the foundation is fixed. Even the landscaping is improved. By the end of the show, there's a dramatic transformation, revealing the once-old house that is now remodeled and fabulous.

In a lot of ways, this is what God wants to do for us as Christians. He wants to take our broken-down, leaky, bug-infested lives and remodel them into lives that are shiny and new. Yet we have to allow Him to work in us. Some of us prefer to stand in the doorway and tell God to get off of our property. We will put the deed in His name, but we won't let Him touch anything.

Friends, this is a great way to stay in first gear. If we refuse the Holy Spirit to work in our lives, we will live in a ramshackle dump until the day we die. God has so much more in store for you!

Letting the Holy Spirit In

It's possible to be saved and never let the Holy Spirit work in your life. I know there are different theological arguments about this, but I've seen a lot of people give their lives to the Lord and then never make a real or lasting change.

The Holy Spirit is the member of the Trinity who is with us all the time. Jesus even told His disciples that having the Holy Spirit with us is better than having Jesus here in the flesh (John 16:7–8). When we take the time to learn to understand when the Holy Spirit is talking to us, we experience the incredible blessing of being continually connected to God.

Having the Holy Spirit is like having a stronger conscience than the average person. I get a distinct feeling in my spirit when I know I'm about to do something I shouldn't—and I know it's the Holy Spirit. I can use these promptings to choose what's right. This shapes my character, keeps me right with God, and transforms the junk in my life.

The apostle Paul put it this way, "And those who are

Christ's have crucified the flesh with its passions and desires. If we live in the Spirit, let us also walk in the Spirit" (Galatians 5:24–25). Just as the Spirit led Philip to the desert (Acts 8:26), Peter to meet with the Gentile believer Cornelius (Acts 10:9–47), and Paul on each step of his three missionary journeys, the Spirit will lead you and me.

Jesus promised us this: "But the Helper, the Holy Spirit, whom the Father will send in My name, He will teach you all things, and bring to your remembrance all things that I said to you" (John 14:26). How encouraging this is! We can be taught and transformed from the inside out.

I'll be honest with you: some people are really good at remodeling the outside of their lives. They have the right clothes, the right hair styles, and the right cars. But if we could get inside the front door, we'd see that their so-called remodeled lives are full of crumbling '70s decorations, rotting floorboards, and peeling wallpaper.

They are like the religious leaders whom Jesus lambasted in Matthew 23:27–28:

> Woe to you, scribes and Pharisees, hypocrites! For you are like whitewashed tombs which indeed appear beautiful outwardly, but inside are full of dead men's bones and all uncleanness. Even so you also outwardly appear righteous to men, but inside you are full of hypocrisy and lawlessness.

What's even worse than this are the people who *act* the right way at church but spend the rest of the week doing whatever they want. They have one face for church and another for home. They sit in the pew shouting, "Hallelu-jah!" and then leave church and cuss people out. They want to get up and preach, but they don't spend time with God. They don't allow the Holy Spirit to show them their sins or remodel their lives. The Old Testament prophet Isaiah minced no words: "...these people draw near with their mouths and honor Me with their lips, but have re-moved their hearts far from Me" (Isaiah 29:13).

We don't want to be in either of those categories. But we'll easily slip into those ways of behaving if we don't intentionally focus on staying close to the Spirit.

Choose Integrity

It's tempting to talk about the importance of reading your Bible and praying here, but I'm not going to. I think the real problem isn't that people don't know their Bibles; it's that they don't follow God with integrity.

For too many of us, church is a place we go to be seen. We want to show off our children in their matching suits and have all the neighbors hear us praying loudly. We spend a great deal of effort to make the outside of our lives look fresh and new while completely ignoring the inside. And that's the part that matters the most!

Jesus put it this way:

> *And when you pray, you shall not be like the hypocrites. For they love to pray standing in the synagogues and on the corners of the streets, that they may be seen by men. Assur-edly, I say to you, they have their reward.*

He also said:

> *Woe to you, scribes and Pharisees, hypocrites! For you pay tithe of mint and anise and cummin, and have neglected the weightier matters of the law: justice and mercy and faith. These you ought to have done, without leaving the others undone.*
>
> **—Matthew 23:23**

What's more important on the car—the paint job, or the transmission? The color of the seats or the condition of the spark plugs? A working radio or a working radiator? What's important to maintain in order to have a car that can get out of first gear (or into it)? Like so much else in life, what's inside dictates how well the outside will work.

Merely *looking* as if the Holy Spirit is working in your life is a sure-fire way to stay stuck in first gear. Only a relationship with Him will allow you to clean up the mess of your life and move into a higher gear. His opinion of you must matter more than the opinions of the people around you.

What the Holy Spirit Isn't

When we are right with the Holy Spirit, our lives don't have to be super Christian-y every second of the day. He isn't asking you to wear a "What Would Jesus Do" (WWJD) bracelet, hat, t-shirt, or bumper sticker so that every person you meet knows that you are a Christian. You don't have to sing hymns every moment of the day.

And when someone asks you how you're doing, you don't always have to have a Christian-y answer.

If you're out playing basketball with friends, play with integrity. Encourage them, laugh at their jokes, and talk about your favorite team. Genuine love is what will win people to the Lord, not merchandise from the Bible store.

If you're on a date with your husband and you've finally got the house to yourselves, do not put on hymns in the background. Don't you dare! Loving your spouse means giving him or her your full attention, listening, carrying on a conversation, and sharing what's difficult in your life. There's a time and a place for "Amazing Grace," but when the candles are lit and things are getting romantic, that is neither the time nor the place!

Nor does the Holy Spirit intend for you to pretend that everything is fine when things are actually not fine at all. A fake smile to cover deep pain is not at all God's plan for you. While you shouldn't give a ten-minute recitation of your problems every time someone asks how your day is going, neither do you have to keep silent about your troubles. Finding a reliable, wise friend, who can listen and point you toward what Scripture says about your situation, is one of God's best ways of caring for you.

The more time you spend reading the Bible, praying, listening to God, and confessing your sins, the closer you'll grow to the Holy Spirit. The closer you grow to Him, the better you'll become at deciphering what it is that God is calling you to do in every circumstance. He will remodel your life. And as the years go by, you won't recognize the person you once were. However, if the desire to look spiritual is more important to you than surrendering to the Holy Spirit is, you aren't ever going to get out of first gear in your walk with God.

First gear is going to church on Sundays and "talking the talk." Higher gears involve:

- Reading and meditating on Scripture daily; memorizing takes these disciplines to another level.

- Serving God through your gifts, both inside and outside the church (more on this in later chapters).

- Listening to the Spirit daily (not only at critical junctures), just as you listen to your spouse, children, co-workers, and friends.

- Worshiping with other believers on a regular basis.

- Pursuing meaningful friendships with godly people.

- Being generous with your time, talents, and treasure, for the growth of the Kingdom.

All these pursuits will shift you from slow, jerky first gear into a forward movement in your walk with Jesus. Or, to put it in HGTV terms, from a fixer-upper to a dream home.

Chapter Two Questions

Question: Have you granted the Holy Spirit access to come in and give your life a makeover? What evidence of change can you see?

_____

_____

_____

_____

_____

_____

_____

_____

_____

_____

Question: Describe the difference between "looking spiritual" and following the Holy Spirit.

_____

_____

_____

_____

_____

_____

_____

_____

_____

_____

Question: If you are following the Holy Spirit, what type of verbal response might you give if you are going through difficulties and someone asks, "How you are doing?" How can a Christian be authentic without being a complainer?

_____

_____

_____

_____

_____

_____

_____

_____

_____

_____

_____

_____

Action: The more time you spend reading the Bible, praying, listening to God, and confessing your sin, the closer you'll grow to the Holy Spirit. Choose one of these four things to focus on in the week ahead. Set a goal to spend fifteen minutes in that discipline each day.

Chapter Two Notes

_____

_____

_____

_____

_____

_____

_____

_____

_____

_____

_____

_____

_____

_____

_____

_____

_____

_____

_____

_____

CHAPTER THREE

Put Down Your Burdens

Be anxious for nothing, but in everything through prayer and supplication, with thanksgiving, let your requests be known to God...

—Philippians 4:6

Picture yourself trying to climb up a mountain to where God's best is waiting for you. It's not an easy climb. You have to use your hands and feet to pull yourself up steep rock faces at times. The path angles upward, and it takes determination to keep going.

Now, imagine you have a backpack full of rocks. Worse, inexplicably, you're the one putting the rocks in your bag—you keep picking them up and adding them to your bag, even as you keep trying to move forward. "My mother is sick," you say, as you lift a stone the size of your hand. "I lost my job and don't know what we'll do next"— you grab another one. "I'm so alone," you sigh, placing another rock into your bag.

It sounds silly, doesn't it? Why would a hiker fill his

bag with useless rocks? But this is exactly what our burdens do for us. Some burdens are put on us by other people, and others are handed to us by life, but some we choose for ourselves. All of them weigh us down and prevent us from moving out of first gear. They might even put us in reverse.

We need to heed the words of Hebrews 12:1–2:

> *Therefore we also, since we are surrounded by so great a cloud of witnesses, let us lay aside every weight, and the sin which so easily ensnares us, and let us run with endurance the race that is set before us, looking unto Jesus, the author and finisher of our faith....*

Honestly, life will contribute enough rocks to our backpacks, with or without our help. Let us throw them all at the feet of Jesus for His freedom and sustenance!

But—can I tell you the truth? Some of us actually like our burdens! More precisely, we like the attention and sense of importance they can offer us. When someone asks about my life and I can tell them about my sick mother, that person empathizes with me and I feel like I matter. That attention can become addictive, but it isn't real.

We are important because God, the Creator of the universe, loves us enough to die for our sins. He can be trusted to care for our burdens. We don't need to hold on to them any longer.

As you're struggling up that mountain, the Holy Spirit will come alongside you and offer to take those rocks out of our bags. He can handle all of our burdens, freeing us to do what He's calling us to do:

> Come to me, all you who are weary and burdened, and I
> will give you rest. Take my yoke upon you and learn from
> me, for I am gentle and humble in heart, and you will find
> rest for your souls. For my yoke is easy and my burden is
> light.
>
> **—Matthew 11:28–30**

Jesus Is Bigger

Jesus is bigger than your burdens. He's bigger than any problem that you're facing. He's bigger than illness, bigger than death, bigger than abuse, and bigger than financial problems. He is able to deal with any struggle or issue that might come your way.

Imagine that hiker turning to the Holy Spirit and saying, "No, thanks. I can do a better job with these problems than You will." What a ridiculous idea! Yet we do that exact thing far too often.

Rather than turning to the Bible or to God in prayer, we complain about our difficulties. Instead of going to my brother who has wronged me, I talk about him to everyone who comes my way. I don't want to wait for God's best for me. No! I'm going to go ahead and marry this man who doesn't treat me well simply because I'm not sure that someone better is going to come along.

How foolish we are! Jesus is bigger, and His solutions are perfect.

Now, let me point out to you that there's a difference between God's perfect will and His permissive will.

Abuse is never God's will, but because He gives us all free will in our choices, sometimes people choose to hurt other people. I am not advocating that you stay in a harmful relationship, especially if you have a safe escape.

But if you are in an abusive situation, this is not God's perfect will, and He will grieve with you, heal you, and help you to overcome the situation. Since He is so mighty, He is able to take these hurts and use them in our lives to draw us closer to Him. He lets us undergo hardship so that we can reach out to those who hurt around us. He permits things that aren't perfect to happen in our lives.

No matter what comes our way, Jesus will never leave us alone. We never have to walk solo through hardships. If you've lived long enough to read this book, you know there are many people who hurt other people, for a variety of reasons. This hurt is not from God; it is the result of a sinful world and sinful people.

But God, in His amazing sovereignty, is able to redeem hurts. He can change our circumstances—He can change hearts that then change circumstances. Whatever burdens are imposed upon us, we can rest assured we are not alone and that the Lord will work all things for our good. As the song says, "Sometimes He calms the storm, and other times He calms His child."[1] We must follow Him, above all else, and respond to His lead, just as Jesus did while on earth.

In the midst of all this, He promises never to leave us alone. Hebrews 13:5b tells us, "For [God] Himself has said, 'I will never leave you nor forsake you.'" Jesus suffered when He was living on this earth. He understands pain and suffering, and He was wrongly accused. If He allows something painful to happen in your life, He promises to be right beside you. He knows what you're going through, and He will use it to His glory.

Dropping the Extra Weight

"You look like you have lost some weight, Bishop!"

"Well, yes, I did, but not physical weight."

When we give our burdens to Jesus, the things that press us down disappear. I'm not saying that you might not still deal with sickness or lose your job, but when you allow the Holy Spirit to take that burden from you, you aren't walking alone. You can turn to Him, hear His voice, and do what He calls you to do.

There was a young couple who lost several babies before their first daughter was born healthy. Oh, they rejoiced over her! Before long, a second little girl came along. The couple thought their hardships were over.

One day, their older daughter became ill, and they learned that she had cancer. This little girl was only four years old, and she had to go through the trauma of radiation and chemotherapy. It broke her parents' hearts to watch her suffer.

Now, it wouldn't have been surprising to see this family grow angry with God. He could have chosen not to allow sickness to consume their little girl, but He didn't. However, the parents chose to trust God anyway. And they went even further than that. They saw the hospital as a place to engage in ministry. There were so many frightened, hurting families in the children's cancer ward, and this family took every opportunity to love each of them and witness to them about Jesus.

God hadn't called them to an easy road. He permitted them to go through a painful experience. However, He was right there with them every moment, carrying their heavy burdens as they climbed. And when their daughter was declared cancer-free, they were closer to God than they had ever been before.

Avoid Contamination

Remember when I told you to think about things that are "excellent and praiseworthy"? That's just as true when it comes to letting go of your burdens as it is regarding how to keep from backsliding. After all, having a backpack full of rocks will definitely encourage backsliding.

There will always be worldly contamination that threatens to keep us from trusting God with our burdens. People in our lives will say discouraging things. Events will happen that disappoint us and make it hard to trust God. We might read bad news or see something devastating on television and find ourselves becoming bitter towards our heavenly Father. Our thoughts are consumed with anger that settles into our hearts, and we start telling people that God has let us down.

We often contaminate ourselves. Difficult circumstances arise, and we cry out to God, "Why me?" We point out all the things we do well and neglect to remind ourselves of what we do wrong. The enemy loves to use contamination as a tactic to corrupt our minds. When we're frustrated, he'll remind us of all the things that are going wrong in our lives. He wants to steal our joy and make us feel incomplete.

How do we avoid this kind of contamination? First, we need to be aware of what problems we are dealing with in our lives. If your boss is being difficult, your marriage is on the rocks, or your car continually breaks down, be aware that these occurrences are likely to lead to worrying. Pray every time you find yourself dwelling on these things. If you can, find a scripture that reminds you that God is in control of the situation.

Every time you start thinking about that problem, picture yourself handing it back to God, then pray for the people involved and repeat that verse. If you're being attacked by the enemy, he will soon stop using that method, since the last thing he wants is for you to pray about the situation ten times a day.

Finally, use wisdom in how you talk about this situation. It's vital that you choose trustworthy people to advise you. You should not constantly complain about the problem to everyone and accept advice from them, because the wrong advice can shape your thinking and change your heart.

This is how you lay your burdens down and let the Father take care of you. This is how you move out of first gear into the forward movement the Lord has planned for you.

WORKBOOK

Chapter Three Questions

Question: Are there burdens and anxieties you are carrying right now? If so, what are they?

_____

_____

_____

_____

_____

_____

_____

_____

_____

_____

Question: Describe the difference between God's perfect will and His permissive will. What truths can you hold on to if God allows suffering in your life?

_____

_____

_____

_____

_____

_____

_____

_____

_____

_____

_____

Question: What does it look like in practice to give your burdens to Jesus? What changes will you see in your life if you truly live in the belief that "Jesus is bigger"?

_____

_____

_____

_____

_____

_____

_____

_____

_____

_____

_____

Action: To assist you in walking through the steps to "avoid contamination," look back at your burdens (question 1). Write down each one, and beside it, write a verse that reminds you Jesus is bigger than that problem.

_____

_____

_____

_____

_____

_____

_____

_____

_____

_____

Chapter Three Notes

CHAPTER FOUR

Shift Your Attitude

*Do not lay up for yourself treasures on earth, where moth
and rust destroy and where thieves break in and steal; but
lay up for yourselves treasures in heaven, where neither
moth nor rust destroys and where thieves do not break in
and steal. For where your treasure is, there your heart will
be also.*

—Matthew 6:19–21

Ben Franklin once said, "To the discontented man, no
chair is easy."[2] That brings a picture to mind of a grumpy
old man who walks up to an amazing chair. This chair is
a recliner with massage and heat, as well as the perfect
amount of padding and support. It might actually be the
most comfortable chair in the world.

However, because this man has elected to become negatively impacted by situations in his life, he finds fault
even with this incredible chair. "The view isn't good," he
says. Moreover, he doesn't like the color of the leather,
and he's hungry.

No matter how much God has done for us and how

much He offers yet to do, some of us are never going to shift out of first gear, because we *don't want to*. We would rather be angry and stomp around than to allow the Holy Spirit to free us of our chains.

There's a strange problem that people who have spent years in prison encounter. Even if their experiences in prison have been dreadful, many inmates struggle to adjust to life outside the jail. While they know the routines and expectations of confinement, they no longer know how to function in the outside world.

The crippled man who had been waiting for healing by the pool in Jerusalem for thirty-eight-years had this type of mindset. When Jesus asked the man if he wanted to be healed, rather than answer what we would consider a resounding "yes," the man simply pointed out that he couldn't move fast enough to get to the healing pool waters (John 5:1–15).

People who have lived their lives in sin don't know how to function on God's terms. But this is why we have been given the Holy Spirit. God's plan is that we will grow closer to Him, and the Holy Spirit will help us to know what it is that needs to change in our lives. But for some reason, we love to cling to our old attitudes and way of living.

After working as slaves in Egypt, the Israelites were finally rescued. God brought them out of captivity and into freedom. And what did they do? They complained about it! In Exodus 16:3, they wished they were living back in Egypt as slaves, because then they had food to eat.

Yahweh's response to them? Quail and manna—food literally from the sky. In Numbers 13, the spies who went into Canaan came back and said they shouldn't take the Promised Land because the enemy was too big and scary. Yet the Lord had told them He would make all their enemies turn their backs and run from the Israelites (Exodus 23:27–28).

God doesn't think this way at all. He has incredible blessings ready to pour out on us if only we will obey the calling of the Holy Spirit. Why wouldn't we do whatever it takes to receive these blessings? Because we don't fully trust Him yet.

In short, we need to shift our attitudes. We need to pursue the practices that will move our attitudes to higher, more productive gears.

Forgive

When we refuse to forgive someone, we hurt ourselves. Our petty, selfish ways hurt us more than they hurt the person we're trying to punish. There's a common saying, "Unforgiveness is like drinking poison yourself and expecting the other person to die."[3] The Lord's Prayer tells us that God will forgive us in the same way we forgive others.

If my forgiveness is dependent on how willingly I forgive others, I had better make sure I am lining up! Forgiveness is not an easy task, but God promises that it is for our good. He even tells us what to do when we are offended. We are to go to our brother who has offended us and discuss the problem, between the two of us (Matthew 18:15).

Sometimes we're so busy holding on to bitterness, resentment, and jealousy that we turn little things into enormous problems. Five years ago, she said something to me with an attitude, and I don't like her anymore. He didn't invite me to his wedding. Her mother doesn't like my mother. I was offended by the way he looked at me.

Is that the way you want God to respond to your transgressions? Suppose God has decided not to forgive your sins. This is precisely what will happen if you do not forgive those who have offended you. Just as Christ forgave those in the Bible who offended Him, we are representatives of Him, and must exemplify the same type of forgiveness with people.

Sadly, sometimes, people cling to a list of wrongs far too long. I've seen women hold on to their engagement rings long after their boyfriends had proven that they were not worthy of these women because of the way the boyfriends treated the women. It's a little old half a carat, but these women are determined not to let it go. They're so busy trying to hold on to a relationship that has ended that they cannot get to the special man God has waiting for them. Forgive, let go, and move on.

I've also seen people make dramatic confessions and extravagant public apologies, yet I know they haven't changed anything at home. I recall an instance when a man got down on his knees in front of me at church to apologize to his wife for an offense that occurred at home. That apology was not for his wife; it was for self-gratification. If you are truly seeking forgiveness, apologize to the person in private. Make it real, and make it count.

An attitude of forgiveness is an attitude akin to that of

Jesus. Pursue it!

Tithing

Bring ye all the tithes into the storehouse, that there may be meat in mine house, and prove me now herewith, saith the LORD of hosts, if I will not open you the windows of heaven, and pour you out a blessing, that there shall not be room enough to receive it.

—Malachi 3:10 *(KJV)*

Often, we do not receive blessings from God as a result of our attitudes regarding tithing. In the book of Malachi, God promises to bless us when we tithe. God is able to meet our earthly needs by pouring out blessings we may not have room enough to receive.

Throughout the Bible, there are times when God asks people to give Him the first ten percent of things. He asked the Levites in the Old Testament to give their firstborn sons to become priests. Farmers were to give the first ten percent of their harvests.

Tithing allows us to partake in something incredible. God blesses those who financially support the church. We are to give a tenth and survive off the remaining ninety percent. If we struggle to make ends meet with ninety percent, perhaps our standard of living is too high, and we need to make some modifications to our lifestyle.

When we tithe, we are trusting that God will meet our needs; we're not putting trust in our money. We're worshiping the God of the universe. That spiritual shift from trusting money to trusting God lets Him move in our lives in tremendous ways.

Now, don't misunderstand what I am communicating. Giving a tenth does not entail receiving envelopes with money from all over the world two weeks after you send a dollar to the church. This is not a get-rich-quick scheme.

God promises to bless you, but He doesn't specify that you will specifically receive a financial blessing. He might choose to allow your son to turn his life around and come back to church. He might provide healing to your body. He might intervene in situations, like protecting you from a horrific car accident or a fire. I don't know how God will choose to bless you, but He promises that He will when you tithe in obedience to Him.

And let's get real here. God requires a tithe from us; it isn't really optional. His will is for us to give to the church, and He will in return bless us. When we do not tithe 10 percent of our gross income, we are actually stealing from God.

Those who aren't tithing are wearing stolen clothing. Everything you own and partake in will be "hot" because you have robbed God. Trust Him to make a way for you to honor and obey what He has commanded of you.

Depress the closed-fist clutch of your manual drive car, and shift your attitude about tithing into a higher, open-handed gear.

Thanking God

Perhaps the attitude shift with the greatest benefit is

this one, and absolutely no one can prevent you from pursuing it: gratitude.

You have the opportunity to choose how you feel about God. Many of us are disappointed that He has not interceded in certain circumstances in our lives to grant specific blessings. We secretly resent Him for not giving us the things that we want.

The innocent missionaries Paul and Silas found reason to sing in a Roman jail. All around you are people who are finding blessings, small and large, in the midst of incredibly difficult circumstances.

Have you ever had a toddler in a car seat while you were driving home? If a baby gets upset, he or she will throw a temper tantrum. The baby will scream and cry while confined in the car seat. Often, the baby is furious that he or she has to sit there. Perhaps, if the baby only knew he or she would be removed from the car seat in a few minutes, the hysteria would cease.

We do the same thing to God, don't we? We become consumed with what we want, and we don't trust that He knows best. We often complain, become fearful, and grumble when God takes longer than we think He should to rescue us from unpleasant situations. All we need to remember is that He is there, working things out for our good. God is in control, and He has had a perfect plan all along.

I believe the antidote to this attitude is thankfulness. Tell the Lord "thank You" for the things He's doing in your life. Do not forget everything He has done for you. He is the One who woke you up this morning—and if that is not enough, remember that Jesus died for you.

When you reflect on your blessings, there is no room for anger and bitterness.

Put Your Past Behind You

There will always be people who want to remind you of who you used to be. That is one of the problems with being in the company of the same people your entire life. You want to make changes, but they continue making statements about who you once were and that you will never change. They may even state that the new you will not last because they know who you really are. Even Jesus, who was perfect and sinless His entire life, was doubted by people in His town—people who knew Him.

> *When He had come to His own country, He taught them in their synagogue, so that they were astonished and said, "Where did this Man get this wisdom and these mighty works? Is this not the carpenter's son? Is not His mother called Mary? And His brothers James, Joses, Simon, and Judas? And His sisters, are they not all with us? Where then did this Man get all these things?" So they were offended at Him. But Jesus said to them, "A prophet is not without honor except in his own country and in his own house." Now He did not do many mighty works there because of their unbelief.*
> **—Matthew 13:54–58**

Regardless of how people feel about you, God has a different story for you. He tells you that your past failures do not automatically result in future failures. You may have failed in the past. That is okay. Do not live in the past because you will not see your future. Do not allow the enemy to use that weapon of defeat to prevent you from becoming the person God created you to be.

God knows you are a sinner, and He has forgiven your transgressions, if you confessed them to Him. Now that you have become victorious over your past, it is your responsibility to not return to it. Why would you go back to the life from which God has delivered you?

Stop beating yourself up, and start focusing on doing better now. The only voice you need to listen to is that of the Holy Spirit. Don't you dare give up a lifetime of living in high gear because people around you have said you will remain in first gear.

What Will Your Treasure Be?

We are all appointed to die one day. The Bible tells us that the time will come when we will stand before God and answer for what we did on this earth (2 Corinthians 5:10). I surely do not want to stand there and say, "I had a really nice house, Lord. I took a wonderful vacation every year. I had forty pairs of Air Jordans." If that were all I could say about my life, I would not have been very productive.

What if my heart were full of bitterness? I would stand before God trying to justify why I could not forgive others. I would have wasted my entire life, and the worst consequence of my actions would be to hear God tell me to depart from Him.

The manner in which we elect to live our lives can provide treasures for our benefit. Earthly treasures will soon be done away with, but heavenly treasures are eternal. Which kind of treasures will you choose?

A life in high gear will be filled with forgiveness, generosity, gratitude, and a positive way of thinking.

WORKBOOK

Chapter Four Questions

Question: Why is forgiveness important for a life in "high gear"? Is there anyone whom you are refusing to forgive?

_____

_____

_____

_____

_____

_____

_____

_____

_____

_____

_____

Question: What does tithing reveal about your heart and your relationship with God? What are your giving habits?

_____

_____

_____

_____

_____

_____

_____

_____

_____

_____

Question: What past mistakes or problems are you letting define you? What does God say about your past?

_____

_____

_____

_____

_____

_____

_____

_____

_____

_____

_____

Action: Examine your attitude. Are you thankful for all God has done for you and given to you? Or do you complain, grumble, and feel yourself entitled to more? Make a list of your blessings. Spend time in giving thanks to God without asking for anything.

_____

_____

_____

_____

_____

_____

_____

_____

_____

_____

_____

_____

Chapter Four Notes

CHAPTER FIVE

Build Bridges, Not Walls

And [Jesus] said unto them, "Do violence to no man, neither accuse any falsely; and be content with your wages."
—Luke 3:14

A trashcan is designed to hold trash, and the trash collector picks it up to dispose of it at the landfill.

This is the same manner in which information tends to travel within our churches. Gossip is actually comparable to trash. It belongs in a waste basket and should be permanently disposed of.

Application of the Word of God is a powerful tool that can minimize confusion and chaos in our churches. The manner in which we communicate in churches is often a major problem. We use our words to build walls between us and our brothers and sisters in Christ. Sometimes we choose to put space between us and someone we dislike. In doing so, when it is time to fellowship or engage in church activities with that particular individual, we discover we have built a wall that will prohibit us from being productive in our gifts.

Do Violence to No Man

> *Speak not evil one of another, brethren. He that speaketh evil of his brother, and judgeth his brother, speaketh evil of the law, and judgeth the law...*
> —*James 4:11 (KJV)*

We can certainly do substantial damage to others merely with our words. In today's society, social media has become a popular source of communication for many. People choose to use this tool to share harmful, and even life changing information pertaining to themselves and others. The entire world can be exposed to misinformation about someone else, as well as confidential matters regarding a person.

Every time we speak harmful words about someone else, we build a wall. Even if it is only an internal wall, in the heart, it still exists, and it brings corruption. Before we know it, we begin to feel as though we are walking through a maze on a daily basis just to survive.

Why can't we simply speak to each other in the manner we would like to be spoken to? It is one of the things we tell our children to do: Treat others the way you want to be treated (Luke 6:31). Yet, we throw that concept right out the window when we reach adulthood. We want everyone to treat us like we are a king or queen, but we want to be able to treat others like they are garbage.

Each one of us has a sin problem and has offended others in one way or another. When we become offended by someone else, we must choose to forgive, not because the other person has apologized or deserves it, but because walls created by a lack of forgiveness are going to keep us from achieving God's purpose in our churches.

And what is God's purpose? To make disciples.

When we are unfriendly and do not portray a welcoming spirit, we prevent people from coming to God. Some people visit our churches and decide not to return because they did not feel welcome. We not only hurt others with unkind words, we hurt ourselves as well.

Worse than that, we disappoint God and interfere with His perfect plan for the church. It would certainly be devastating to stand before God one day and hear Him say that our attitude towards others negatively influenced someone's decision to come to Christ.

What would be the end result if we were to defend others and refuse to partake in gossip? What would happen if we were to strive to treat others the way we would like to be treated? Would we not have a different atmosphere in our churches?

Neither Accuse Anyone Falsely

There is a game we like to play with the younger generation. Everyone makes a long line, and the person at one end of the line whispers something to the person next to him or her. That person repeats what he or she has heard to the next person, and the whispered sentence travels down the line. By the time the last person has heard the statement, it is completely different from the initial message. How often do we talk about people when we are not even certain that the information is factual? When we participate in gossip, walls are being built.

However, when we choose not to listen to such fabrication, we build bridges instead. When we courageously tell gossipers that we elect not to engage in gossiping, we build bridges. When we kindly excuse ourselves from such conversations, we build bridges. When we value building God's kingdom, we build bridges.

Be Content with Your Wages

Another major problem in churches is jealousy toward other people in the church. We often spend a significant amount of time attempting to compete with one another. Looking good becomes more important than being good. We tend to assess our strong areas and compare them to others who are weaker in those capacities. Sadly, we convince ourselves that we are, therefore, superior to those individuals.

The Bible says that there's one Maker of heaven and earth (Isaiah 45:18). He said that the poor shall always be among us (Matthew 26:11). Who are we to think we are better than someone else because we have received more than the next person? More than likely, this person would prefer to gain additional blessings, but it is not his or her season yet. Christians should never boast about blessings and favor they have received on their lives.

In most instances, the things we lord over other people are things we cannot even control. They are typically God-given talents or gifts that we are not even worthy of receiving.

Be content with what God has given you, and do not boast about it when He blesses you with more. The best is yet to come. What we have on this earth is temporary and will not determine whether or not we make it to heaven. If God decides not to entrust you with millions of dollars, He has good reason. Trust Him, and grow closer to the Holy Spirit, so that you can choose to be content with your blessings.

Comparing ourselves with others can lead to corruption. We must accept one another as God has accepted us, despite our imperfections. We must receive one another as the father received the prodigal son—with open arms of love, because the joy of one returning home from the corruption of sin should be celebrated. We must learn to apply to our lives what the apostle Paul did: in any state, to be content (Philippians 4:11).

Build Bridges

Shift your mind, shift your mouth, and shift your attitude. Our mouths reveal what is really in our hearts. Our conversations reveal what is really going on inwardly.

Begin by being more selective with what you allow to enter the gateway of your mind. You must then shift what you express verbally. Discuss issues you have encountered only with the person involved. If someone comes to you with an offense you have caused, humble yourself and listen. Search your heart and go before God. Repent, apologize, and move onward.

Finally, adjust your attitude. Rejoice with those who rejoice; mourn with those who mourn (Romans 12:15

NIV). Do not sulk, gloat, or dwell on the fact that he or she did something underhanded and does not deserve the promotion.

Christ reconciled sinners to God. As His ambassadors, we are in the same bridge-building, barrier-breaking, reconciliation business. We can do this in slow lurches, like we are in first gear, or we can portray generosity, kindness, and love, to make real progress in bringing about the will of God to be done on earth as it is in heaven.

Choosing to love people in our churches is not always easy. We often step on each other's toes and get our feelings hurt. God calls us to give grace, as we have received grace. Our churches will never get out of first gear if we are not building bridges.

WORKBOOK

Chapter Five Questions

Question: What type of communication builds walls, and what type builds bridges?

_____

_____

_____

_____

_____

_____

_____

_____

_____

_____

_____

Question: Have you ever been the person about whom others were gossiping? Have you been unfairly judged or looked down upon? What doubts and emotions did it cause? How can you avoid doing the same thing to others?

_____

_____

_____

_____

_____

_____

_____

_____

_____

_____

_____

Question: What are the dangers of comparison? What does God say about it in 2 Corinthians 10:12?

_____

_____

_____

_____

_____

_____

_____

_____

_____

_____

_____

_____

Action: How will you respond the next time someone comes to you with "garbage" and tries to get you to take it? Write out and memorize some key phrases that will help you to graciously but firmly stop gossip and backbiting from spreading.

_____

_____

_____

_____

_____

_____

_____

_____

_____

_____

_____

Chapter Five Notes

CHAPTER SIX

Choose Love

Though I speak with the tongues of men and of angels, and have not charity, I am become as sounding brass, or a tinkling cymbal. And though I have the gift of prophecy, and understand all mysteries, and all knowledge; and though I have all faith, so that I could remove mountains, and have not charity, I am nothing.

—1 Corinthians 13:1–2*(KJV)*

Love is a word that we throw around a lot, especially in church. We say that God is love (1 John 4:8), but what does that really mean? Some people tend to use the word love to captivate others' minds for their own personal gain. Other individuals do not demonstrate characteristics of love at all. When some try to love as God loves and others do not, this creates a difficult situation. It becomes extremely challenging to shift to the next level.

What Love Is

First Corinthians 13:4–13 gives us a full description of

love, "Love is patient, love is kind. It does not envy, it does not boast, it is not proud. It does not dishonor others, it is not self-seeking, it is not easily angered, it keeps no record of wrongs. Love does not delight in evil but rejoices with the truth. It always protects, always trusts, always hopes, always perseveres" (NIV).

This is who we are called to be, as well. What would our churches be like if there was no envy, no bragging, no rudeness, and everyone was working for God's glory? The church would be a place where people feel welcome and never want to leave. It would be a safe place for the broken, the sick, the poor, the outcasts, and the lonely. It would be a place of kindness, healing, and freedom through the Truth of Jesus.

If true love were in the equation of marriage, the spouse who tried to live according to Biblical principles would no longer receive less in return from the other party than what he or she was contributing. If true love existed, no longer would a man feel obligated to purchase a ring he cannot afford, simply to prove his love.

Beware of False People

Unfortunately, many of our churches are not like this. We are too busy with our lives, our activities, and our families to have time to love others in a real way. Our words of love become false when we do not back them up with loving actions.

I think the word *charity* in 1 Corinthians 13:1–2 (KJV) can be interpreted as love in action. When we tell everyone that God is love and that we are His people, then we must love like He does, or we are just like tinkling cymbals. They just sound good, but do not have much effect. When we say we are Christians, we must love people sincerely; otherwise, we are speaking falsely.

There are people who want to charge money to prophesy and pray for people. If people are really working for God, there should not be a fee attached to the gifts He has so freely given unto them for His glory.

If you want to avoid being false, let honesty dwell within your heart. Make it a practice to check on others, and help them if they have a need when you are in a position to assist.

What Love Isn't

Now, I know there are some people out there who may read this and think, "I am not loving *her*." I've seen you come in during the service and the usher leads you to three good seats next to someone you dislike, so you choose three bad seats in the corner where you can hardly hear the sermon.

There will always be people you find hard to love. That is just how it is sometimes. But you are not excused from showing these people love. Love is not comfortable all the time. It is not always going to fit into your schedule or require only what you are willing to pay.

Love does not work if your pride gets in the way. If you are too busy to forgive someone, you will never learn how to love him or her. Gossiping, arguing, insulting, and fighting are not examples of love.

World-Shaking Love

Bobbi had no interest in Jesus. She had a difficult childhood and never had a single positive interaction with a Christian. In fact, when she was approached by Christians, she was often rude to them.

She went to live with her fiancé several states away from home. Not knowing a single person there, she started to spend time with her fiancé's friends. Little did Bobbi know, her fiancé had joined a card-playing group and befriended a Christian. This friend invited the couple to come out for dessert with their community group and then to participate in game night.

Before Bobbi realized it, everyone she knew was a Christian. Even though she was not quick to turn her life over to Jesus, the loving care of these friends went a long way towards repairing her painful history with churchgoers. By the time Bobbi and her fiancé moved back home, she was much closer to entering into a relationship with Jesus than she had ever imagined.

If we truly want to shift our churches into high gear, we need practical acts of love. Whether it is by helping people to move, watering their plants while they are away, or inviting them over for dinner, we can always show people God's love in ways they had never imagined.

First gear is loving our own, those like us, and those we like. It is loving with conditions and expectations.

Shifting gears will require that we love our enemies, those who are not like us, and even those we do not like. It entails loving without conditions, and, in short, it is the high-octane love our Savior demonstrated towards us.

How can you show love to someone today?

Chapter Six Questions

Question: Would you describe your church as a loving place? Why or why not? How can you help to impact the environment in your congregation?

_____

_____

_____

_____

_____

_____

_____

_____

_____

_____

Question: Why is it so important for love to have practical action behind it? Give examples of love in action versus love that is simply professed.

_____

_____

_____

_____

_____

_____

_____

_____

_____

_____

Question: Read John 13:35. How does love win people to Christ? Share an example from your own life or the life of someone you know.

_____

_____

_____

_____

_____

_____

_____

_____

_____

_____

_____

Action: Commit 1 Corinthians 13:4–7 to memory. Make a list of each of the attributes of love. Note how God displays that attribute to you. Then note how you can show that attribute in practical ways within your family, church, or community.

_____

_____

_____

_____

_____

_____

_____

_____

_____

_____

_____

Chapter Six Notes

CHAPTER SEVEN

Shift the Church for the Next Generation

That which we have seen and heard declare we unto you, that ye also may have fellowship with us: and truly our fellowship is with the Father, and with his Son Jesus Christ.
—1 John 1:3 *(KJV)*

People have a tendency to declare that children today are different. They were saying it about my generation when I was a child, and we say it now about our children. The fact is, the world keeps changing, and the children of each generation adapt to what their parents have provided for them.

The struggle within most churches, however, is that we don't like change. Church becomes a part of our personal culture. If we were reared in the church, we remember what it was like when we were young, and we became accustomed to our upbringings as standard practices.

When I was a child, we did not have children's church.

We sat next to our parents and were chastised if we misbehaved in church. We did not have marriage or credit counseling seminars. If we had a problem, we talked to the pastor and he gave us instructions on how to approach the situation.

Church is not just about what transpires within the walls of the edifice. Christians serve as disciples who are commissioned to tell the unchurched about Jesus by spreading the Word abroad. When Jesus spoke about "the church" in the New Testament, He was referring to the people who were following Him. Church is what happens throughout the week as well.

Embracing the New

This message is not just designed for church leaders; it is for everyone who wants to be obedient to the will of God. Nothing harms God's plan for the church more than a congregation that refuses to obey the vision that has been set forth by the visionary or pastor. We, as Christians, should learn to embrace change as the church shifts into the twenty-first century.

God is not pleased when members fight against and resist instructions by the man of God. He gives the pastor a vision with specifications for that particular church, and members need to simply adhere to direction from the pastor. God has placed him as overseer, and the people are to follow him as he follows God. If the pastor decides not to follow God, the people are not, at that point, obligated to follow him.

Letting Go of the Old

I have witnessed some of the worse disagreements in churches over matters with absolutely no relevance. It is amazing how we never disagree about things we want to change in our personal lives: furniture, cars, hair color, homes, and other material items. Therefore, we should not disagree when God gives purpose for change in the body of Christ.

The church needs to embrace baby boomers, Generation X, and millennials alike to attract them to the church in order to promote growth—because it is crucial that everyone feels welcome, wanted, and loved in the body of Christ. Churches in America are closing at an alarming rate because we are reluctant to do what needs to be done so the next generation can carry on after us.

We will never shift from first gear if we are clinging to the old and fighting to keep ourselves comfortable, instead of adjusting to welcome new people. If our eyes are centered wholly on ourselves and our needs, we are not looking out for hurting people around us whom God has called us to love.

When visitors come, the church should have visible strategies in place that promote growth, change, an action plan, order, structure, effective communication, and most of all, love.

If our churches do not welcome visitors, we are not growing God's kingdom. If younger people do not feel welcome, eventually all of the old members will age and no longer be around.

To be honest, we also need to let go of past hurts. Visitors do not become members of churches where congregations are full of people who are grumbling about, and with, each other. I am not saying that past hurts are not real and still painful.

There are a lot of people who have been hurt by those in the church. I can't say that I blame them for how they feel. Believers can be pretty judgmental at times. Wouldn't it be a beautiful thing if church members would focus on Jesus instead of themselves, and on loving others instead of getting their way?

As Jesus said, "By this shall all men know that ye are my disciples, if ye have love one to another" (John 13:35). In a world full of people who are hurting and people who commit hurt, what an irresistible attraction our love for each other can be! Our focus as believers should be on growing closer to God and advancing His kingdom.

WORKBOOK

Chapter Seven Questions

Question: Why is it important for churches to change as culture changes? How do you usually respond to the idea of changes in your church?

_____

_____

_____

_____

_____

_____

_____

_____

_____

_____

Question: Give examples of helpful (though perhaps un-comfortable) changes versus sinful, unbiblical changes that a church can make. What makes the difference?

_____

_____

_____

_____

_____

_____

_____

_____

_____

_____

_____

Question: What are some of the things—physical and spiritual—that can cause people not to feel welcome at a church? Are you personally welcoming to guests who visit your congregation?

_____

_____

_____

_____

_____

_____

_____

_____

_____

_____

_____

Action: Take time to dialogue with people younger than you about what is important for them in church. (If you are under thirty, talk with people who are older and ask them the same question.) How can your church reach the next generation?

Chapter Seven Notes

CHAPTER EIGHT

Shift Your Mindset

Every way of a man is right in his own eyes, but the Lord weighs the hearts.

—Proverbs 21:2

Do you ever get tired of dealing with other people? Tired of their mistakes, tired of their criticisms, tired of their interfering in your life? We live in a time when we are highly critical of other people—and we have social media, where we can post our opinions steadily.

We spend so much time fussing about other people and what they are doing. Then we spend all sorts of energy worrying about what someone else will think if we do this or that. We are busy avoiding this person and remembering to be mad at that person.

Unfortunately, this sort of behavior is rampant in the church. I know I've talked about this a good deal already, but it's such a problem that we must make sure we address it thoroughly.

We need a mindset shift in our churches. We need to

shift our criticism off everyone around us and take reasonable responsibility for ourselves. I can't control what anyone else does, and complaining about it certainly won't help.

The apostle Paul told us to regard ourselves with "sober judgment" (Romans 12:3 NIV). We are to look first to the perfect example of Jesus, then into the mirror to judge—soberly—how our image reflects Him.

This doesn't mean we dismissively "live and let live," without qualification. But our interactions with others in the church should be seasoned with salt, grace, and encouragement, even when the things that need to be said are difficult.

We are responsible for showing love and encouragement to each other. However, keep in mind, we are only responsible *for* ourselves—how are we using our gifts, time, resources, network, experience, passions, and hearts for the Lord?

Use Your Gifts

I would certainly love to be gifted at administration. I know that seems silly to many of you, but it's true. I can preach, and I can lead people, but I am not gifted when it comes to managing office responsibilities.

Our church's secretary, though, is a gifted woman in that area. She is able to keep track of things, stay on schedule, and answer the phones with a cheerful voice. Her abilities are truly remarkable to me.

Now, I'm sure there are a few people who think her job isn't that important. However, she allows the church to operate smoothly. God has called us to a number of things, and this woman works tirelessly behind the scenes to help us all do what we've been called to do.

No, you might not have a singing voice that allows you to get a solo in the choir. You might not have the gift of patience to work with toddlers in the nursery. But God has equipped you with a certain gift that He intends for you to use for His purpose.

It's easy to spot people who are using their God-given gifts. They flourish where they are planted and bless everyone around them. It's remarkable where these people appear. Sometimes it's where you'd expect: as teachers in a school, as pastors in the pulpits of churches, as singers on a stage. But sometimes you find a greeter at Walmart who lights up everyone who walks by with her friendliness. Sometimes it's a mechanic who makes every car he touches run better.

God has given you a gift. As you grow closer to the Holy Spirit, He'll direct you toward your gift and will help you find a place to use it. Often, we are simply drawn to certain things. We find ourselves enjoying them or coming back to them repeatedly over the years. Maybe you love to volunteer to park cars, or maybe you have a talent for making the church website better. Perhaps you love to meet with hurting people in the church.

Don't discount your gift. It's not like anyone else's, but it is what God has given you. Spending time wishing you had a more glamorous gift is a waste. Get your eyes off your desires and focus them onto God's desires instead. I love the way Kurt Jurgensmeier puts it: "Who we are is God's gift to us; who we become is our gift to God."[4]

Shift your mind from trying to lift yourself up to lifting God up, instead.

Join the Team

Church is a place where people must work together. Romans 12:4–8 tells us that we are all parts of one body. If you wake up in the morning and your eye says, "I'm not going to work with your brain today," you're in trouble. Your foot and your elbow aren't going to get upset and start refusing to spend time with your leg or your arm. Your shoulder isn't going to decide to go play golf instead of joining the rest of you at church.

The first part of joining the body of Christ is showing up. I think that people who grow up in the church have a real advantage here, because attending church is part of their normal routines, and a part of their personal culture. Not being involved in church feels funny to them. Raising our children up to feel this way is a great gift we can give to them.

I find it odd that people won't ever miss work because they see the advantage of being on the job, but they are happy to miss church since they don't think it matters. God is the one who provides your needs, not your paycheck. You need to make sure you are on good terms with the Lord—the one who can protect you from anything, the one capable of blessing you until you can't hold it all, and the one who has loved you enough to die in your place.

The second benefit to joining the body of Christ is submitting to leadership. I know many people who have the desire to lead, but until you can follow, you will never be ready to lead. Even though I'm the pastor of my church, I still submit to the authority of those above me.

The third part of joining the team is to learn to communicate well. We've talked about this a lot already. Speak to people as though God is sitting right there listening, which He is. Respect other people's opinions and remember that your way of doing things isn't the only right way. Listen and ask questions. Remember that the people around you are human beings with souls, who have just as much baggage to drag around as you do.

Look at Your Own Sin

There seems to be some confusion between looking out for your brother and spending your time criticizing everything he does. The Bible calls us to care for one another, to look out for the poor, and even to confront each other when we are sinning.

Unfortunately, some of us have taken that to mean that we get an opportunity to be nosy and spend all our time and energy looking for what's wrong with the people around us, and then complaining about it.

I've found that what helps me most is to spend the majority of my time focusing on my own sin. If I'm busy asking the Holy Spirit to help me to see where I need to improve, confessing sin when I find it, asking for forgiveness, and working to not continue these sinful habits, I don't have much time left to be upset about what other people are doing.

As my mother used to say to me when I was quick to

point out my siblings' misdeeds, "You worry about you, and you'll be too busy to worry about your brothers!"

In addition, when we see more clearly that we are each sinners, we have much more grace to give to the people around us. I might not struggle with alcoholism, but I know myself well enough to know that if I'd been in the same circumstance as that fellow over there, I'd probably be one, too.

Everything that I do well is thanks to God—His work and His blessings in my life. It has little to do with what I've earned. If I were given everything I've actually earned, I'd be in a sad state, indeed!

When it comes to people hurting our feelings, we must first examine ourselves. Ask yourself: *"Am I being too sensitive? Is that person speaking from a hurt experienced in his or her own life?"* Understanding my own sin means that I don't have to be shocked when someone sees that I'm not perfect.

It also means that I know what it's like to say something I regret or that I said without thinking. I don't have to be angry with that person, because I know the full measure of grace that has been given to me, and I am ready to give a little to that person as well as to myself when I'm in the wrong.

Fix Your Eyes Upon Jesus

We need to shift our minds off ourselves and onto Jesus. Lifting ourselves up will never have eternal benefits like lifting Jesus up will. If our churches are full of people who are more concerned about their own lives and their own agendas than they are about the body of Christ, we will stay stuck in first gear.

A car stuck in first gear—like a believer stuck in first gear—weaves this way and that way because the driver is busy looking at all the other cars, all the other cool toys the other drivers have, and the sporty coupe he or she used to have.

A car that's cruising down the road smoothly is a car driven by someone who is focused on the road ahead, using all the tools at his or her disposal to continue successfully. A shift in mindset will take a driver as far as a shift into a higher gear—and the same is true in your life as a follower of Jesus.

WORKBOOK

Chapter Eight Questions

Question: In what areas have you let your irritation or contention with others distract you from God's plan for you and your church?

_____

_____

_____

_____

_____

_____

_____

_____

_____

_____

Question: What is your spiritual gift? What are some skills and talents you have? How can these be used for God's glory in your life right now?

_____

_____

_____

_____

_____

_____

_____

_____

_____

_____

Question: What are the benefits and blessings of being connected to a local church? Rather than focusing on others and your disappointment with them, where should you keep your focus?

_____

_____

_____

_____

_____

_____

_____

_____

_____

_____

_____

Action: Take a spiritual gifts and/or personality assessment. Talk to one of the pastors at your church about how you can be involved using your gifts to help make a difference.

Chapter Eight Notes

CONCLUSION

A Life in High Gear

But if we walk in the light as He is in the light, we have fellowship with one another, and the blood of Jesus Christ His Son cleanses us from all sin.
—1 John 1:7

A race car driver pulled up to his place on the track. All of the competition stopped to admire his car. The paint job was out of sight, the tires were the best on the market, and the car purred. All the cars lined up, and the drivers began to rev their engines, ready to start the race.

The flag was dropped, and the drivers popped their cars into first gear, peeling out and onto the track. However, when the other drivers shifted to second and into third gear, the driver of the fancy car stayed in first gear. He maxed out at fifteen miles per hour and could only watch as the other cars lapped him again and again.

"Why am I not going faster?" he growled. "My engine is state-of-the-art. This is the best car on the track! What's wrong?"

Throughout the text, we have looked at how staying in first gear will keep us from living the life God intends for us. You won't grow spiritually or truly experience God's blessings if you don't shift into a higher gear.

If you never make the changes to shift out of first gear, you aren't going to make any progress. You'll live the same life you've lived up until now. Your church will have the same problems that it has always had. The choice is yours.

Change begins with small steps. Choose your friends wisely, guard your mind, and keep from backsliding. Grow closer to the Holy Spirit and let Him take your burdens. Invest in treasure in heaven that will last forever (Matthew 6:20).

Change your church by building bridges, forgiving those who've hurt you, and loving each other actively. Prayerfully trust your church leadership and strive to welcome new people. Focus on making yourself better.

You know what life is like in first gear. Progress is slow; it's bumpy. Shifting into high gear will take work. It requires, well, *shifting*. It requires change, and it requires risk—if you shift carelessly, you might stall. It requires a different speed, a different feel, and more focus.

It will require you to keep trying when you fall down. You might even have to let go of relationships that are pulling you back.

But a life in higher gear has extraordinary benefits: more progress at a higher speed. There are few thrills like the open road at a steady hum of the car, with joy in both the journey and the destination.

So changing your mindset, guarding your mind, laying

down your baggage at the cross, forgiving, letting go of the past and straining toward what is ahead (Philippians 3:13)—it's all worth it.

Are you ready? Begin today to fight for the life that God intends you to have!

REFERENCES

Notes

1. Scott Krippanye. "Sometimes He Calms the Storm." Lyrics and music by Benton Kevin Stokes and Tony W. Wood. *Wild Imagination*. Word Records, 1995. See also: The McKameys, "Sometimes He Calms the Storm, and Sometimes He Calms Me," quoted in Georgia Purdom, "Sometimes He Calms the Storm, and Sometimes He Calms Me," *Dr. Georgia Purdom* (October 21, 2010). https://answersingenesis.org/blogs/georgia-purdom/2010/10/21/sometimes-he-calms-the-storm-and-sometimes-he-calms-me.

2. Lemay, J. A. Leo. *Printer and Publisher, 1730–1747.* Vol. 2 of *The Life of Benjamin Franklin*. University of Pennsylvania Press, 2006, p. 195.

3. Williamson, Marianne. Quoted in Patrick Mabilog, "Forgiveness: Why Holding On to That Grudge Will Only Hurt You," *Christian Today* (March 31, 2016). https://www.christiantoday.com/article/forgiveness-

why-holding-onto-that-grudge-will-only-hurt-you/83008.htm.

4. Jurgensmeier, Kurt. *Biblical Faith*. Vol. 6 of *Knowledge of God*. Training Timothys, 2012, p. 280.

About the Author

Bishop J. W. Jasper Jr. is the son of the late Rev. John W. Jasper Sr. and Mrs. Mammie Jasper. He was baptized in his youth at Sunshine Church of God in Christ. Rev. Jasper accepted his calling to the gospel ministry in 1991 and served faithfully for more than twenty years.

Bishop Jasper attended Houston Public Schools and is a graduate of Phyllis Wheatley High School. After graduating high school, he attended Inner Baptist Theology Center in Houston, Texas, where he received a Bachelor of Theology degree in May 1994.

In 2001, Bishop Jasper was appointed assistant pastor of New Light Baptist Church under the leadership of the late Pastor D.A. Easley. He served faithfully in this position for three years, until Pastor Easley appointed him to be the new senior pastor.

The anointing that rests on the life of Bishop Jasper has allowed the evangelism, ministry, fellowship, and discipleship activities of the New Light Baptist Church family to overflow. Bishop Jasper is committed to taking God's Word to a hurting and lost generation as he allows God to use him as a vessel to help build people of character and purpose.

Bishop Jasper is married to the love of his life, Angela Jasper. He is the proud father of six children: Lacy Robins, Xavier Bloodsaw, Jana Rodgers, Sharlishia Valentine, Javonta Jasper, and John Jasper III. He has also been blessed with five amazing grandchildren: Jayden Robins, Jaycie Robins, Jermarion Rodgers, Zoey Bloodsaw, and Zaria Bloodsaw.

About Sermon To Book

sermontobook
.com

SermonToBook.com began with a simple belief: that sermons should be touching lives, *not* collecting dust. That's why we turn sermons into high-quality books that are accessible to people all over the globe.

Turning your sermon series into a book exposes more people to God's Word, better equips you for counseling, accelerates future sermon prep, adds credibility to your ministry, and even helps make ends meet during tight times.

John 21:25 tells us that the world itself couldn't contain the books that would be written about the work of Jesus Christ. Our mission is to try anyway. Because in heaven, there will no longer be a need for sermons or books. Our time is now.

If God so leads you, we'd love to work with you on your sermon or sermon series.

Visit www.sermontobook.com to learn more.